THE COMMUNICATION FRIENDLY SPACES APPROACH™

Re-Thinking Learning Environments For Children And Families

Elizabeth Jarman

Published in 2013 by ELIZABETH JARMAN®
ISBN: 978-0-9927091-0-5
www.elizabethjarmantraining.co.uk

"We need to challenge the historical stereotypes that often exist around the way that learning environments are set up for children, blending new understanding of learning styles, how children really learn and their preferred contexts so that our environments can be responsive and dynamic."

Elizabeth Jarman

Acknowledgements

This updated publication has been triggered by our ongoing thinking, discussion, research and work with hundreds of professionals, all striving to create really effective environments for children and families. Thanks to everyone who contributed their ideas, images and case studies.

Special thanks to Rosemary Albone for helping me to collate this evidence into a document which will help you to challenge some of the historical stereotypes that still exist around the way that environments for children are 'expected' to look.

I hope that you are inspired to re-think your environment, using the Communication Friendly Spaces Approach™ (CFS™) within your context!

Futher details about Elizabeth Jarman can be found on the back cover of this publication.

Foreword

We know that experiences in children's early years significantly shape their future development. All of us want to get it right for children, to give them the best possible start.

Over the past decade, we have discovered so much more about the significance of early brain development, healthy attachment, the dependencies, crossovers and influences within developmental areas, the importance of authentic learning and the 'essential glue' that warm, interested and engaged adults can provide for children and their families.

As professionals working with babies and young children continue to adopt an attitude of enquiry within their practice, creating the space, time and place for all of these critical components to mix together has been identified as key.

This publication is not about the benefits of den building, or carrying out a cosmetic makeover of a learning space, or perhaps trading plastic for wood. On a much deeper level, it offers an underpinning approach, backed up by research, ideas and current thinking to help you to explore the way that the environment you offer can set the scene for meaningful learning and connection to take place.

Introduction

This handbook aims to inform, remind and embed the constant need to review and re-think the role the learning environment can play, wherever that is and for anyone working with children and their families. The CFS™ Approach focuses particularly on creating environments that support speaking and listening skills, emotional well-being and physical development.

The CFS™ Approach has been used in schools, early year's settings, public spaces and community places globally. In this updated version there are case studies featured throughout to show you how the CFS™ Approach has impacted positively. This handbook is not a definitive guide of 'how to do it', but a collection of research, case studies and observations for you to interpret and use in your own context. Think of it as a sign-post within your journey to improve the conditions you create for learning.

From a CFS™ perspective, we know it's essential to challenge the historical stereotypes that have led to the creation and acceptance of learning environments for children that:

- dismiss or don't even consider what the space looks and feels like from a child's view
- ignore the negative impact of poor physical layout and access
- accept clutter; increasing and overwhelming quantities of poor quality and developmentally inappropriate resources
- disregard the evidence base relating to the use of manageable colour
- forget to consider the effects of excessive noise and continuous artificial light

The CFS™ Approach needs to be intrinsically embedded into your practice and connected to your pedagogy, as it's not an 'add on' but a should sit at the core of how you want to make learning possible for your children.

Creating a learning environment to suit the current needs of your children and families requires on-going monitoring, changes and adaptations as children's preferences and interests develop. Continuous observation and responsive action is key. Routine, rigid termly or semester based changes will inhibit responsiveness and reduce the opportunity to seize that critical and magical moment when learning really connects.

Using this handbook will help you to understand more about the impact that the physical and emotional environment has on communication skills and why it's so important to plan it so very carefully. We hope that this revised edition will inspire you to find ways to improve your learning environments by:

- Researching
- Reflecting
- Connecting
- Experimenting
- Noticing
- Adapting
- Responding

Blending all of these areas together, aligned with careful observations of children's learning preferences and acknowledging the role of the adults working in learning spaces is important if we want engaged learning to take place. It's as simple as that. It's time.

Use the CFS™ Approach and get started!

Definitions

It's been hard to agree on one term that covers the wide range of professionals working with children and their families, regardless of the context.

We've settled on the term practitioner and we hope that within it you recognise the complex skill set, essential attitudes and attributes that make up these highly skilled roles.

The same issue cropped up when we were thinking about location and context and so we've included a range of references to different places where we interact with children and their families; regardless of the location when we talk about the learning environment, we mean all areas, inside and out.

Throughout this handbook we have added professional prompts to trigger your thinking.

For example: "Stop, notice and consider"

How is your concentration affected when you are in this busy space? Where in your setting would you prefer to go when you want to think about something or chat with someone?

Scattered throughout the handbook are a series of quotes, research summaries and hard data designed to help you connect and reflect.

We know that these nuggets of information can be helpful when you are sharing the CFS™ Approach with others.

For example: "Did you know?"

Bronzaft and McCarthy found that children on the quieter side of a school next to an elevated railway had reading scores higher than children on the side exposed to the train noise.

The Communication Friendly Spaces™ Approach

For too long, the quality of children's learning environments has not always been enough of a priority. Environments have often evolved over a period of time as equipment has been purchased and then added to (and further added to without any associated de-cluttering). Indoor spaces might have been decorated and then parts re-painted with little regard to colour schemes. Outside spaces might lack the same care and thought given to layout and resourcing as inside. What we have ended up with in many cases is a one-size-fits all offer, often full of bright clashing colours, crowded wall space, poor storage, overwhelming amounts of unused resources, too much plastic and artificial equipment with, an abundance of hard chairs and lots of tables, poorly lit environments and spaces where noise is an ever constant companion. The time has come to blend new thinking about the potential of environments with better understanding of how children learn so that we can create really great environments that really do set the scene for effective engagement.

It's important however, to recognise that adopting the CFS™ Approach can be very challenging for some practitioners, settings, families and visitors as quite often the learning environment transforms visually into a very different space.

"For many teachers their environment is still a blind spot: unchanging, unchangeable and beyond their control - an obstacle that they must work around, rather than a tool to support and enhance their practice."

Design Council, Learning Environments Campaign Prospectus, 2005, p18.

"Strengthening children's early language development is the golden thread in improving quality and outcomes for young children. The size of a child's vocabulary at five is a key indicator of later academic success. That is why it is so important to support practitioners in developing communicative environments so that children can build their stock of words and, quite simply, talk more."
Sue Ellis

Regardless of location and circumstances, improving children's speaking and listening skills is high on the agenda for us all. We know that young children learn in a holistic way and so a key role for us is to help establish connections between ideas and concrete experiences that are representative of things that matter to them from their immediate families and communities as well as from a wider perspective.

Developing communication skills does not take place in isolation- they need the context within which they are relevant in order to help children assimilate and then practise their new knowledge and skills. This development is best encouraged by offering children environments in ways that help them sift and sort through what matters to them, in manageable ways and with opportunity for repetition, re-visiting and processing time, with sensitive, informed support from practitioners. We agree with this definition of effective conversation skills:

- The ability to listen, absorb and understand what is being said
- The understanding to be able to follow the thread of a conversation and add to it
- Use and add vocabulary associated with the topic
- Ask questions that extend the ideas shared, listen to the answers
- Confidently express opinion, even if it differs from the majority view

- Appreciate the ebb and flow of a conversation, drawing others in to contribute and not overtaking
- Develop skills to pick up the non-verbal parts of interacting with others
- Building healthy relationships through engaging in respectful dialogue together

For these skills to develop well, children have to feel secure and have a sense of belonging. The environment can play a really important part in creating this climate.

 Are your children seeing these components of healthy communication skills in the people around them? Are your communication skills worth copying?

The CFS™ Approach takes a holistic view of the learning environment focusing on the following three areas working in harmony together; no one area is sufficient on its own:

The Physical Environment

Focuses on the layout of space, the flow of movement, the physical transitions that take place, the way in which space affects behaviour, confidence, communication and cognition, the amount of softness in the environment, links to home and cultural representation, the use of colour and light and the impact of noise.

Resources

Here the focus is on scale, quality, developmental appropriateness and purpose of resources and equipment. We also note the way that resources are stored, offered to children and engaged with by children and adults alike; resources are not just for children.

The Adult Role

Celebrating the positive impact that warm, significant, caring adults have on children's emotional health and well-being, their attitude towards learning, relationships and the related impact on speaking and listening skills.

Each of the three areas affects how a space works, feels, facilitates, scaffolds and enables and they are of course, interrelated.

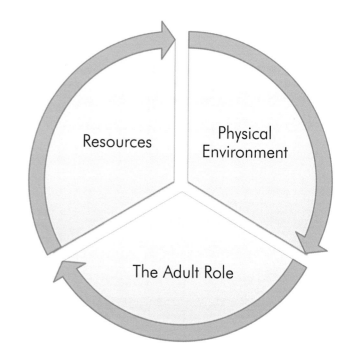

As we have shared CFS™ key messages with practitioners and families the same two significant points are regularly highlighted as fundamental:

That the learning environment must connect with the underpinning pedagogy of the setting.

We need to think about the learning environment as a pedagogical space not simply somewhere that learning happens randomly. It requires intentional thought and attention to detail. A shared vision around what people want for children is key. Being able to explain this vision jargon free, so that everyone involved has a shared understanding is really important. Can you explain what you want for children in your setting? The physical space should then be informed by the vision. There is so often a mismatch between what people say they want for children and what the environment makes possible. Make sure this is all fully aligned in your context through reflection, discussion and auditing.

If your vision is to encourage children to be independent yet they are overwhelmed by too many resources on a developmentally inappropriate scale, is your learning environment truly supporting independence?

The second significant point:

It is critically important to observe the way that children are interacting with the learning environment.

There are times when we are only focusing on what the children are doing and don't pay enough attention to where they are choosing to spend time in the setting. How are your children using the space available to them? Where are the places that they seek out and prefer to be? What is it about this space that draws them? Size? Position? Place? Where are the 'dead' spaces? Which children prefer to learn outside? How does your environment take account of and facilitate this?

 The way that a learning environment is set out can influence children's behavioural response. If a room has a long 'runway' then children are likely to run! Look at your layout. How does it influence flow of movement and the places where children gather?

"What we are talking about here fundamentally shifts our traditional thinking in terms of how and why we present certain resources, furnish and layout our space. It may be that as a setting you recognise that a rethink is in order.

As a priority, each setting must ensure that they are clear about the philosophy they are promoting and how that is translated and lived out through the environment.

This review can have a catalytic effect and help to freshen and redefine aims- all of this is helpful, although at times scary!" Constance Tyce.

 Could you confidently share your pedagogy with others?

Does your approach:

- *encourage independence?*
- *offer children opportunities to interact with each other, or to be alone and uninterrupted?*
- *provide secure and respectful links to children's families, homes and communities?*
- *ensure that learning opportunities are relevant to the children because they occur in meaningful contexts?*
- *encourage a balance between action and stillness, interaction and quiet?*
- *share the great learning that is taking place and the contributing steps along the way?*

"We invest time in observing the children and their developments, but we also need to contextualise this view. The environment is key in setting the scene for actions, behaviour, interaction and consequences.

Be clear about what you want for children in this space and ask yourself does this space enable that to take place?

We all need space to think, space to be alone, space to get away from it all and to be ourselves. Sometimes that involves others and sometimes it doesn't."
Rosemary Albone

The Child's View

Our role as practitioners is to be an early advocate for children and to seize opportunities to involve children in exploring experiences. Understanding their perspective should help to shape our own perspective too. One of the key reminders of this is a quote from the renowned Artist Henri Matisse

"Il faut regarder toute la vie avec des yeux d'enfants."
"All, your life, you must see with a child's eyes."

Consistently whilst sharing the CFS™ Approach through training events, conversations, research and social media networks people tell us that once they start to view their learning environments from the children's perspective many of their previously long- held assumptions are challenged and often squashed as they realise for example that areas that might look inviting to them as adults take on a very different feel when they are viewed from a child's height. Resources that were organised and offered in ways that adults felt would encourage participation and engagement very often cannot be clearly seen, often a very basic reason for non-engagement!

Following the exploration of the environment from the child's perspective, we regularly hear practitioner feedback of spaces feeling too large and overwhelming. There can often be a lack of small spaces, spaces that offer containment, places to withdraw to and watch from.

 Take photographs of your learning environment from both an adult and a child's perspective. Review them and acknowledge the differences in appearance, accessibility and appeal. Link this thinking to your observations of how children are using your space and accessing resources for learning. Does your imagery help you to understand the appropriateness of your space?

Many practitioners suddenly realise that previously by not experiencing their space as a child would, they have overlooked what was effectively 'staring them in the face'. If we are to truly place children at the centre of what we do, we need to consider their perspective at all times.

The power of a photographic image is a useful tool in identifying how learning environments are viewed as a very young child. The difference in height creates individual perspective and ignoring this fact means that a lot of the effort that adults put into the creation of a learning environment can be wasted if the child's view is not thought about.

An area that was set up as a baby garden for children in those very early developmental stages of crawling, walking and becoming more independent featured a range of grasses, plants, small trees and bird feeders. It had been defined by using some rush roll fencing and the planting had been left to grow wild creating height, fragrance and movement.

The nursery took some additional photographs of this space, this time from the approximate height of the children who would be using this area and this is the result. The practitioners realised that suddenly this space took on a whole new appearance and perspective; what had once looked inviting, interesting and worth investigating (potentially on your own), now had the potential to be somewhere that independent investigation might not be so appealing.

The long grasses, whilst wonderful to clamber through and feel brushing your face, now might be adding to a sense of anxiety. Where do I go in, how do I find my way back out again and what's in there?

Above: The adult's perspective

Below: The child's perspective

What do the children think?

Children are active researchers, commentators and are perceptive and frank about their experiences and their ideas for change. We need to nurture climates that encourage them to let us know honestly what they think. But be prepared! The children's ideas may initially seem unworkable or might challenge the way you've done things for a long time.

Over the years that we have been working with the CFS™ Approach, this has been one of the most revealing and debated questions raised. 'Whose space is it anyway?'

To ignore 'pupil voice' at any age of child- is a serious flaw in developing the pedagogy of a school or setting. If we state that we intend to enable children to be confident communicators, independent decision makers and effective problem solvers and then do not encourage them to tell us about their experiences within the learning environment that aspires to facilitate this, then we are failing them and in turn fooling ourselves. Just as we expect to be consulted about decisions, which affect us, so should the children and as ambassadors for this, we must ensure that we facilitate it with care and respect. Children at all ages are not simply passive receivers of information but active learners and how we respond to this will affect our practice and the outcomes for children.

Using consultation when working with CFS™ brings a multi-layered set of benefits. The process of consultation contributes to increased self awareness and self confidence, a feeling of contributing and that your voice and ideas matter; additionally the level of positive engagement and opportunity to speak, listen and be heard are all healthy communicative activities.

In a recent project with primary schools in the Wirral, UK, we consulted extensively with boys across the age range about places they liked and places they didn't like around school. Here are some of their comments:

"I like going in the classroom, because I've always got someone to talk to like Declan and Joe."

"I like going to dinner because I'm always full."

"I like going in the lilac room and learning about new words with Barbara."

"I don't like the toilets because they are very smelly."

"I don't like the playground because it's busy and noisy and I get hit by the ball."

"I don't like going to assemblies because they're far too long and when I have to get up, my legs are killing me!"

 What do your children think about your environment? How could their feedback inform changes you make?

- *Are all of your decisions about the learning environment based on quick conversations and brief reviews of the children's activities and progress?*
- *How regularly and meaningfully are you consulting with the main users of the learning environment- the children? How would they answer the question "what do you like about this space?"*
- *What value are we placing on children's views and opinions and what ways are we accessing them?*
- *Next time you visit another school or setting see if you are clear about their pedagogy simply from observing the learning environment. What do you notice that is both subtle and overt in the way that they intentionally demonstrate their core values?*
- *What would they notice in your space on a reciprocal visit?*

Find out more

Find out more about consulting with children in a wide range of contexts, by researching these documents and papers:

http://www.ncb.org.uk/media/124848/no.7_consulting_children_about_play.pdf

http://plan-international.org/where-we-work/africa/publications/consulting-with-children/

http://www.pupilvoicewales.org.uk/nursery/get-involved/ways-of-consulting-with-the-under-5s/

http://www.earlychildhoodaustralia.org.au/every_child_magazine/every_child_index/engaging-with-childrens-voices.html

www.children.act.gov.au/documents/PDF/under5report.pdf

www.schoolzone.co.uk is all about redesigning the classroom environment

An interesting short paper 'Pupil voice is here to stay!' by Professor Jean Rudduck. http://www.serviceschoolsmobilitytoolkit.com/resourcedownloads/staffroom/bpv_theneedtoinvolvepupilvoice.pdf

CFS™ Considerations for the Physical Environment: Space Matters!

It's often useful to think about the many parallels in terms of the spaces that we use as adults. The choice of where to sit in a coffee shop is a good illustration. Heading in there on your own with a magazine to read and a need for peace and quiet sets your radar in action to seek a space that provides these conditions. If the space is empty, it's easy to align your needs with the places available. As the cafe fills up, your choices become limited and the chances that your needs will be fully met are minimized. We may still seek out a space there, but the time that we spend lingering beyond the drinking of the coffee is likely to be shortened. If we wish to share that space with a friend, likewise we seek the conditions to meet our requirements and if the match is good, we stay.

Think about how you would respond in this situation. Would you:

- Like to sit with your back to the wall so that you have good visual opportunities to see what's happening but still feel protected by the solid wall behind you?
- Choose to sit in a secluded spot where you won't be seen or heard, perhaps seeking some rare privacy?
- Position yourself at the first table free, so that you don't have to walk through the busy space?
- Make eye contact with anyone else in the café?
- Prefer to have a few moments to yourself reading through your magazine and enjoying your latte before feeling more confident to look up and survey the room?
- Any other preferences or behaviours that you know you do in this or similar situations?

Take a moment to think about your response and the parallels you could draw with your observations of children and ways that they interact with space. What about that child who usually finds themselves a space that they can watch from until they are ready to join in?

What about that child who wriggled into a corner and made themselves comfortable there whilst listening to a story? Why does that sofa positioned by the door seem to be the place that new parents/carers in your setting gravitate to when they first start coming along with their children?

The physical environment aspect of CFS™ incorporates a review of the following key areas:

The use of space

Thinking about layout, developmental appropriateness, flow of movement, engagement and concentration

Storage and resource management

How resources are stored and made accessible to children, developing independence, quality and quantity of resources

The effects of noise

Creating conditions for listening and engagement

Informed use of colour

Ensuring the physical environment encourages concentration, positive behaviour and is visually inclusive

The impact of light

Using lighting effectively

Use of Space

"When we talk about the environment we need to consider the structure and layout of the building and the outdoor space, the resources available to us and how they are used. Many settings suffer from well meaning architects whose general view was that 'children are small, so let's make everything dinky'."
Lesley Staggs

We've yet to hear a practitioner tell us that they work in the perfect space! What constitutes the perfect space anyway? We all have different ideas about this as would the children. In fact, ask your children and see what they think! Historically, more emphasis has been given to storage, ease of keeping the space clean , 'control' through formal layouts, lots of display boards, more adult-directed activities with a focus on inside and less consideration of outside as a place to facilitate learning.

With contrasting ideas and opinions about what the space is for, who it is for and what its intentions are, it's no wonder that on occasions we don't really 'get it right'. It's time for a re-think. If we want learning to happen, we need to create really informed places for it to take place and a one size fits all approach, is most definitely not the answer.

 Are there really any restrictions on the way you arrange your environment or are they self-imposed or historical?

Where do your values and knowledge about the environment emanate from? Are you swayed by images in educational supplier's catalogues, an assumed image that others 'expect' your environment to look, feel and sound like?

Sometimes we 'self-impose' restrictions or arrange the setting in a specific way to accommodate practical routines, the shape of the space or for the ease of adults in the environment. By doing this we could minimise learning. The environment needs to facilitate and enable rather than 'contain' children's learning.

In considering the use of space, our starting point has to be based on observation and really watching where children are placing themselves, noticing where they gravitate to, where they re-visit regularly, areas they like to transport resources to and settle while they investigate them. Noticing where speaking and listening is taking place, where children are spending relaxed and highly engaged time.

It's also important to remember that speaking and listening takes place within an emotional context. When we review the learning environments that we have created we need to acknowledge that for some children their emotional balance, which can be incredibly transient, may contribute to their need to verbalise or not, their preference for who is present, the confidence which they draw on to respond to others communication and how on occasion, speaking aloud can draw unwanted attention, for those children who present as less confident, can be an almost paralysing fear and have serious implications for their public communication skills.

For some children, wide open space is not always considered somewhere 'emotionally safe'. Being able to access somewhere small, perhaps contained and private, somewhere to observe from, can be very necessary for children, especially as they make the transition into a setting or school from home or even from one space to another within the setting. High ceilings, hard floor surfaces and no visible boundaries represent an openness that is hard for children to navigate in an emotionally confident way. Reviewed from their perspective, the size of the space is often disproportionately large and could be difficult to navigate. If this is your observation, it's an indicator that an audit of your space is required to align it more closely to the developmental needs of your children.

Children's preferences in terms of contexts for learning i.e. the place that they chose to spend time in, and for speaking and listening, in terms of space, may not be static. Some children are much more confident communicators when they are on the move and so when we think about creating Communication Friendly Spaces™ we need to keep this in mind so that all children have their learning preferences met.

"Improving your learning environment should only ever be undertaken as a result of careful observation of what the children are doing, how they are using their space, and what preferences they are revealing. "

Rosemary Albone

Remember that children do not always need adults to initiate conversation, particularly when they are engaged in imaginative play. We can all re-call observations where child-led imaginative play has provided wonderful examples of the interchange between children. This can be encouraged by careful use of space and creating areas where children feel secure, not obviously overlooked or overheard. This creates conditions which enable them to enter into their play free from a sometimes inhibiting adult presence. Their language skills will benefit from the opportunity to openly express creative ideas and develop this play as they listen and interact with their peers.

Consider the way in which children are going to use the space aligned to their preferences.

What will they need in the space? Do they really need tables and chairs in the area or is that an adult fixation? Are we predetermining what has to happen there? Be reflective in your considerations and face the challenge of taking risks confidently in terms of offering different spaces which may not initially look 'traditionally educational' but careful observation of their use will soon identify the amount of learning that is taking place there.

Using the opportunity to visit early year's provision and schools whenever possible, we are often struck by the contrast between the time and care given to think through the layout, organisation and permission the children have inside, in relation to that of outside space. Sadly, too regularly we see outside space that is a mixture of poor storage, overflow from indoors, a lack of definition, bland open space, adults hovering over children's play policing their actions and nowhere for children or adults to sit together.

Conversely we are often also delighted to observe children transporting resources and equipment to locations they choose, children accessing spaces and places creatively, more open-ended uninterrupted play, emerging independence, physical challenge and a freedom to make choices that is sometimes not as forthcoming indoors.

"The best classroom and the richest cupboard is roofed only by the sky" Margaret McMillan, Nursery Education Pioneer 1914

The positive influence of Forest and Beach Schools in the UK has done much to change attitudes towards the value of outside and the endless possibilities that it as a context for learning can offer. Additionally the encouragement to offer continuous provision, where children have access to inside and outside fluidly according to their preference throughout their time in that session actively puts children in charge of their own playful desires and space choices. These types of shift changes in the sector, not only in the UK but worldwide, has done much to support more child led decisions within in play and should be heartily encouraged.

Do you have subconscious attitude about the way that the inside and outside is arranged, organised and how children are enabled or permitted to move and play within those spaces?

Are your children more able to transport and make changes to their environment outside but perhaps not inside? Why is this?

Having professional conversations about things like this are really important in establishing a shared understanding and consistent approach.

"View your setting as a whole space. Consider every nook and cranny and think about how it could be used effectively. Of course, this includes outdoors. Lots of settings still under use their outside space or don't consider of to be worthy of thought and planning. Consequently children use it differently, often not constructively and yet it is a rich source of opportunities for language skills.

Start by reviewing one area and then let this be the trigger to influence a review of your whole setting. Each part may be very different and so it should be if you are truly basing your ideas on the children."

Lesley Staggs

Arriving at your setting: Transition

Put this publication down and if you are in your setting, go outside and then walk into the building as a parent/visitor would, imagining you are new to the site. If you are not there, visualise this. Notice what the layout, signage, decoration, level of information (text and visual) indicates to you. How welcome do you feel, how do you know where to go, who could you approach, what does their body language indicate to you about your presence, how is your culture represented, how is your child and your aspirations for them shared with you in this space and how do you get in?

Now repeat the exercise and consider things from a child's perspective. What does the space look like, smell like, offer, how does it support your transition in? Where do you go if you just want to watch for a while before joining in, are there resources to interact with that look familiar enabling confident early engagement, how quickly can you see a familiar adult, are they sitting on the floor indicating that you can join them and they will give you time to warm up to being here, what resources and images make sense to you, how does the size of the space feel- too big, high ceilings, lots of noise, can your family member stay with you for a while until you are ready to engage?

So many questions to consider! Use them to audit your space and practice. Refresh your memory of being new here, or a visitor/user of the setting.

Our knowledge of children and families continuous transitions should help us to think about the learning environments that we create. Smooth transitions help to settle children and adults anxieties and enable them to seamlessly cope with the next change. For some children and adults, it's as simple as finding the way in, locating a place to leave your bag, gently starting the day in ways

that match your personal energy level or tolerance for noise, need for nutrition or a thirst for company.

Thinking about the physical aspect of CFS™, the way in which we arrange space, furniture, resources and people must focus on helping those initial transitions take place in ways that reduce any anxiety, make separation more tolerable (for both children and their significant adults), and make connections between home and the setting.

Case study

Jackie, a home based childcarer from Weymouth, UK was acutely aware that the transition process into her setting first thing in the morning or at the start of a session for her children and their families impacted on the rest of the day. She had noted that the initial separation between the children and their parents was equally hard for both of them. She considered ways in which she welcomed everyone and how her practice indicated that for the children it was ok to stay with her and for the parents it was ok to trust Jackie with the care of their children.

Jackie used opportunities within her physical environment to indicate that everyone was welcome even when her front door was shut- each day she chalked a different message on her doorstep to tell her families that she is thinking of them. In terms of healthy emotional attachment, this approach connected people and reminded them that they mattered, that they were being held in another's mind.

Jackie also closely observed the behaviours that she saw demonstrated by the children and adults when parents were dropping them off with her. She noticed that this separation could sometimes be made more difficult for the children by the often unconscious non-verbal signals that their parents were giving them. This had resulted in some children finding it hard to settle. Jackie talked openly with her parents about this and introduced a short song session that everyone now does to signal that it's time to go.

"I know that as children hear and participate in that song they psychologically move into my care and that parents also at that time, make the shift in their thinking and hand their children over to me- both emotionally and physically. Introducing this has enabled these critical transitions to be smoother for everyone"

Magda, a mother of twins who attend Jackie's setting added *"Jackie understands how it feels to leave your children and how hard that is. We now sing together and then my children know that it's time to stay and play. Because I know that they are settled I can then leave without worrying and that is better for all of us"*

Many children develop an almost ritualised approach to arriving and settling into early years settings. They might make a habit of touching specific bricks in the wall, stroking a particular plant or talking to a favourite photograph as they walk in and this part of their routine is essential to helping them anticipate arriving and managing transition in ways that make sense to them and offer the emotional support of transitionary objects.

This can be particularly relevant for children accessing care outside of the home for the first time as they start to use adaptive behaviours to help them manage this very significant transition. Adding unusual points of interest on the route in can engage families immediately.

Children's personal possessions or 'transitional objects' can relax and emotionally bridge home to setting for children during transitions and are helpful in enabling them to manage uncertainty. They become a physical representation of home and should be, where possible accessible throughout the day.

Find out more:

"The psychology of stuff and things" Christian Jarrett on our lifelong relationship with objects.

http://www.thepsychologist.org.uk/archive/archive_home.cfm?volumeID=26&editionID=228&ArticleID=2313

Screening and a Sense of Privacy

Making large spaces feel smaller can help children achieve a sense of proportion that they may not experience in high ceilinged, wide open spaces. This is just as relevant outside. Creating screening that gives the effect of creating a room within a room can break down areas, adding definition. This type of informed change can help children concentrate better and spend longer in areas, which impacts on their engagement levels. It also offers some privacy, permitting children to gain control over who is listening to their conversations and interactions. Privacy for children is we know, a contentious issue and one that is often clouded by safeguarding issues. It goes without saying that keeping children safe is of the highest priority, but what is worth exploring is the amount of privacy children have, or intentional space for them to be on their own if they choose to.

When we ask professionals what they think about intentionally giving children a space where they can have privacy we get a mixed response. 'Yes, we know that it is important,' they say 'but how does that fit with us needing to see children at all times?' It's a tricky question and one that delves deep into our personal beliefs about children and their rights. It also requires a sensitive compliance with safety. Think about your own needs, in relation privacy:

- Do you like your own company?
- Do you actively seek your own company even for a few minutes each day?
- How would it make you feel if you couldn't access some privacy?
- What does this make you think about in relation to children accessing privacy?
- Do adults have a right to privacy where children do not?

When we talk about screening, it's worth remembering that even the sheerest of materials can give the illusion of privacy whilst still giving full visual access to those outside of the space. Screening off an area with voile, netting and thin materials still creates the sense of walls or protection from the world beyond the fabric and for some children that provides the ideal conditions to use their voices and vocabularies more confidently than when they feel or can see that they are being listened to.

CFS™ that we have observed on our travels often have an element of screening and practitioners report that when they observe children's speaking and listening skills within these spaces they are often amazed at the vocabulary range, the verbal confidence, the dynamics of different groups of children communicating together, the increase of home languages spoken and an increase in children with English as an additional language using English more regularly, testing it out, rehearsing and noticing how others react to their emerging skills. Feeling screened off from others can create a liberating effect and one can reducine shyness.

Screening provides a place to withdraw to, to access stillness, calm, somewhere to watch from. It also helps to minimise visual distraction from activity around that area and contributes to children's ability to focus

 Where do you go when you want to rehearse a new word, to say it out loud?

Case Study

The team in this Nursery in Ohio, audited their outside space as a review of their offering for their children aged 3 plus. They were expanding the opportunities for talk in their outdoor space and wanted to develop options that offered support for speaking and listening, stillness and calm.

Their location backed onto a residential area, which often created a distraction and they also identified during their observations that there was no seating provision in the garden.

First they hung a sheet on the wire fencing to screen off the distractions and to delineate the area, they then added a semi-circle of seating logs positioned to facilitate listening, eye contact and sharing. Simple, effective and immediately of interest to the children who gathered there to share stories and conversation.

Once the CFS™ was installed and in use, the practitioners noticed that the babies and young children in the adjoining garden were showing a great deal of interest- hanging on the fence to watch! Expert practitioners then realised that this type of space was needed in the baby garden too and they replicated it with a smaller semi-circle of logs.

Screening and a Sense of Privacy

Here are some examples of different sorts of screening, some temporary, some permanent.

The Need for Softness

Many schools and settings are increasingly reviewing the use of softness in their environments. When we use the term softness we mean the use of cushions, soft flooring, sofas, rugs, throws, cosy small chairs and spaces where children can feel gently physically nurtured. This is especially important for children who spend very long days in settings and need somewhere to retreat to, for a rest or time alone.

Traditionally, 'learning' has been associated with with tables and chairs, resulting in 'hard environments'. Research from Harvard University has made strong links between softness supporting emotional independence. Take a look around your space and identify where you would gravitate towards if you wanted to get comfy and re-charge for a while?

This message is as relevant for adults in the environment so it's worth reflecting on the types of spaces that we need too. Arriving home after a long day at work often our immediate need is to just take a few minutes out to make the transition between one role and place into another. Armed with a warm drink and a new magazine, we don't generally opt for a hard kitchen chair in harsh lighting, we tend to gravitate towards a sunny open space or a welcoming sofa, enjoying the enveloping softness it offers.

Why then do we all too often only offer hard seating spaces for children or expect them to read or work on utilitarian table and chair arrangements when we as self-selecting adults would not choose that for ourselves? We need more softness in our settings to ensure that comfort is a priority to suit learning preferences, increase concentration and to nurture.

Softness in the form of sofas and cosy chairs, rugs and cushions can make links between home and the setting - a situation which home based childcarer's are already catering for instinctively. For families accessing your services these add not only a level of comfort but a non-traditional approach to furnishing a learning space; one that is much more aligned to a meeting space without the formality of traditional schools spaces. Adopting this way of thinking has been very successful in many family centres by engaging methods that have purposefully considered the impact of the physical space in a learning environment that wants to increase family engagement.

You can find out more about this by accessing our website: www.elizabethjarmantraining.co.uk

Comfort is equally relevant in the outside space too. Adult seating is often lacking and this promotes a very different set of behaviours from practitioners as they spend time outside with the children. In the absence of somewhere to sit, adults often 'police' the space, walking around monitoring the behaviours rather than engaging in the holistic experience.

Audit your outside space for places where adults and children can comfortably interact together and where the ergonomics of the space encourage this to be sustained for periods of time so children get the sense that adults will stay- sadly quite a treat in today's busy world.

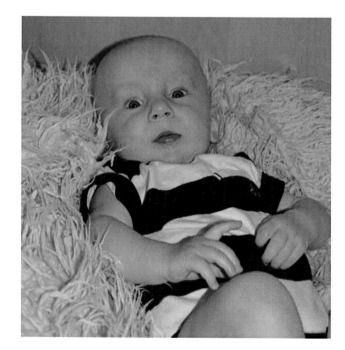

Small Spaces

Group based settings globally have one thing in common- they tend to encourage group based behaviour and interaction. We are all in agreement that this is a key skill; it underpins social mobility and encourages high interpersonal sensitivity to evolve. There is a need for balance when designing a learning space, to incorporate smaller spaces so that you don't have to be with too many other people all of the time. Many children develop their speaking and listening skills within the context of small groupings, a handful of key relationships and in situations where they are less exposed to large groups. As you look around your outside and your indoor space, notice the small areas that children have transported resources to, or places where they have squeezed themselves into, to create some 'personal space'. It is likely that they have chosen or even created for themselves, small spaces. That could indicate to you that you need more small spaces in your learning environment.

Remember also, that small spaces can be moveable, flexible and even human! That small space on your lap creates a wonderful nurturing environment.

Small spaces can also intentionally be created for one. This might take some thinking about, as historically in group care based settings we focus on areas that accommodate more than one child typically. Initiating a straw poll amongst a few people, investigate what they think about spaces for one; their responses might surprise you.

Many people tell us that they recognise the need for time on their own as an adult but had not consciously thought about it for children. As they do begin to mull it over a range of advantages and potential disadvantages emerge.

Enclosure

Many children feel a sense of security when they are in areas that are fully or partially enclosed. The screening of the enclosure doesn't need to be solid in material terms, but create the illusion of a covering/separation from the rest of the space. Feeling that you are somewhere semi-private indicates that you cannot be overheard and for some children that is an incredibly enabling condition with regard to them being freed up to use their skills whilst not feeling under any level of 'surveillance'. Net, thin muslin type materials, camo netting, sun shelters, tents, wind breaks and sheeting all work well when they are draped, used to create screening or clamped onto tables, chairs, fences and trees to delineate a space.

Partial enclosure works well in lots of cases, offering the semi-privacy of an enclosed space combined with easy visual access for supervising adults.

In buildings with high ceilings it is worth investigating what this space feels like to children, from their height. Whilst to adults it often appears light and spacious, from a child's perspective it can feel overwhelming scale wise and noisy.

Lowering the ceiling by using light materials can be effective in creating the illusion of a more proportionate feel and again offers a zone which is more suited to the physical height and perceptions of children.

When creating an enclosed CFS™ for very young children and babies, we should be mindful that some babies in particular are reluctant to enter spaces when they are not able to see a way out. Where babies enjoy being part of a small group or indeed an opportunity to interact on a one to one basis, the use of a small space can enhance this engagement deeply as it provides a level of security, reduces distraction and offers a secure base to visit and return to, particularly when emotional refuelling is needed.

A Place to Talk for Babies contains a a wide range of different context and situations where practitioners, babies and their families spend time.

Outside Spaces

The freedom and movement associated with outside space creates exactly the right conditions for many children to use their communication skills most confidently. When we think about why this might be, it is evident that outside feels less formal than inside. There is also an association with a lack of permanency outside and for some children this frees them to simply communicate and represent their ideas more freely. Practitioners who have used their outside spaces to focus on communication observations have reported an increased use of linguistic skills, particularly in boys and have been amazed at the breadth of vocabulary noted and the confidence in terms of communication delivery.

The way in which adults communicate outside often differs from when they are with children inside. Think about that in relation to your practice. Adults can often just keep on the move and sometimes don't stop for any length of time. How do you support, extend and engage in talk within this preferred context for many?

Auditing our own practice within this context may identify some development areas.

Does your communication vary when you are outside? What drives this?

Using the outside area imaginatively has already been highlighted as critical, as there are so many different sorts of opportunities to facilitate speaking and listening in this context. Also, it's the preferred learning space for so many children. Be prepared to alter your thinking about using the outside. It is simply another part of your space, not a different add on to inside and yet we still see many schools and settings treating this area as a fair weather friend!

Gardens and outdoor spaces often lend themselves naturally to smaller, interesting spaces with bushes, trees, steps, fences and sheds offer some full or partial screening, shade, privacy, edging and definition to a space. We know that when children go outside they often gather in spaces that we might prefer them not to initially; for example they will explore behind the bushes, round by the bins, at the bottom of the garden just out of sight and gather on the bottom step or behind the doors to the shed. As you observe carefully you may notice that this is where talk takes place! They may well be engaged in intense conversations feeling that they have a sense of ownership of their space, a little privacy, a natural gathering spot and somewhere that they can relax.

When we think about very young children and babies outside, security is of course a consideration, not just in terms of their physical safety but their emotional safety too. The combination of small contained spaces with warm caring adults is a recipe for healthy communication and emotional well-being.

Navigation of the Space

Whilst the amount of movement outside is liberating for many children, there are some who view the possible activity of outside as something to be anxious about. Thinking back to the example we explored about our choice of seat in the coffee shop, some people opt for the nearest free table to settle at because it prevents them having to walk through the other customers. They might settle there and do some people watching before feeling ready to move to a place that suits them better.

For lots of children, a place to 'watch from,' particularly outside can be a helpful transition space giving them a safe area where they can observe the level of activity, how things are done around here and join in when they are ready.

Creating a CFS™ outside, or may be near to a doorway so that children can access it quickly and without fuss is an ideal.

For some children staying where they are, watching and taking it all in will be enough, for others using this transitionary space as a stepping stone to greater, more confident engagement outside works well too. Secure spaces, carefully positioned to return to can also help children to navigate new spaces, which is a really important consideration.

Consciously thinking about positioning is also important when arranging furniture, to promote speaking and listening skills and non-verbal communication skills. When benches, chairs, stools, cushions, blankets, tents and buggies/strollers and wig wams are positioned, think about the view that is provided, does it facilitate eye contact for the children, closeness so that everyone can hear and protection from too much flow of movement so that talk can take place uninterrupted?

Case Study: Smiley Faces

Observing children's social and emotional development enables us to tune into situations that cause children stress and tension. Noticing that one of their children was demonstrating a very clear preference for having her 'own space' and finding it hard to share highlighted a need to support her to find ways to establish and sustain positive socialisation with the other children in the group. Sensitively they acknowledged that this might just be needed for short bursts of time combined with enabling her to access her own space, responding to her needs.

Using their observation, the team gave themselves time to professionally reflect on what they already knew about the child and how she responded to space, her learning preferences and their philosophy. They created this CFS™ for her, featuring her own voile wigwam, carefully positioned with its opening facing an identical wigwam. This inspiring CFS™ offered her a space of her own where she could manage her emotions and need for control, whilst still interacting with other children and not becoming concerned that they would want to come into her area. The success of this CFS™ lies in the way in which the team interpreted the child's developmental stage, interests and emotional responses. The positioning of the openings of the wigwams was central to its success.

The Floor as a Learning Space

Whilst hard floors can represent an uncomfortable space for many of us, for some they are just a natural learning arena. To be able to spread out your chosen resources, stretch out your body and become deeply engaged in play is an easier task for some children when it's on the floor. Delineating floor spaces can be helpful in 'protecting' play and resources as well as creating defined zones. Thoughtfully placed mats and rugs, baskets of resources and plants can all indicate edges and suggested visual boundaries helping children navigate their way around the space, resecting others activity and creations perhaps. Being able to work with resources, leave them and return to them are important facets of evolving play, helping children take time to become deeply involved, to develop play ideas and recall events.

Case study

Noticing the flow of movement in your learning space will indicate to you the ways in which play and engagement can be enhanced or disrupted. In this setting the team reviewed their layout and spent some time observing how children were using the space and where they interacted with particular resources. Some of the use of resources was influenced by the positioning of storage and by the practical layout of furniture. The observations illustrated that the location of the wooden blocks and train track was affecting the depth of engagement of play and the associated communication as it was situated in a thoroughfare. The children wanted to work creatively with the blocks for sustained periods of time, leaving and then returning to them, was impacted by the location as other activity continually interrupted this play and physically moved the blocks. Additionally they needed to be moved and cleared away to permit other resources and activities to be accessed.

The team realised that in order to support the play and deepen the engagement level, a re-think was required. Talking with the children identified what they felt about the situation and captured their ideas. A decision was made to re plan the space to move certain pieces of equipment to free up and protect more floor space in an area not so open to interruptions.

As a result, subsequent observations noted an increase in sustained play, rich communication, additional dynamic groupings and the children creating tangible strategies for expanding their creative input. The ability to leave the resources out and for the children to return to them and find them in the same state as when they left them was an important element in this.

Do you routinely put specific types of resources on the floor and others more table-based? Why? What messages are you sending?

Protecting individual activity is important too; using small mats that children can self-select and choose where they want to locate themselves can work effectively in giving them independence and decision making opportunities.

Containment

If you've observed the children that you work with squeezing into impossibly small spaces, clambering into containers or emptying resource boxes and getting into them then you are seeing containment. The feeling of being contained offers a physical comfort and boundary and this 'holding' can be a very reassuring position. Many children and adults too, often seek a place where in particular their backs are covered making sure that they cannot be approached from behind. This makes a great deal of sense when we think about feeling safe, relaxed and out of danger. Communication skills are enhanced when the speaker or listener can tune in to the conversation without external distractions. Containment creates these conditions and is able to be managed and sustained by the child independently- as long as well-meaning adults don't disrupt the opportunity! Contained CFS™ can be created that are just big enough for one or for a small group. Children don't have the same sense of protocol regarding personal space and generally appear to be content to be squeezed into a small space together. However, contained spaces can also be created for one but situated alongside each other to extend the opportunity for communication to take place, acknowledging the stage of parallel play.

Very often the fascination of a contained space is the fact that adults don't comfortably fit in and children enjoy this slice of adult-free space. Practitioners should note how this affects behaviour and engagement and also question how often we give children adult free time.

Remember, all of these examples demonstrate the importance of considering simple but informed environmental changes. The way in which furniture, resources and activities are arranged and positioned can either encourage or discourage social interaction and participation. Maximising the use of outdoors as a valuable learning space is also critical.

Storage and Resource Management

This is often a real discussion point when we work with delegates. People never seem to have enough storage! It often strikes us however, that the person telling us about the issue is almost metaphorically weighed down by their overwhelming clutter and sense of visual overload! Some of us are life's natural recyclers and hoarders! We use something, spot some potential resources whilst we are at the supermarket, on holiday or walking home and start to gather them. Before we know where we are our cupboards are full, containers are spilling over, we run out of cupboard space and start searching around for other places to situate our ever increasing collection of 'stuff'. Often we end up using the children's space as storage, which impacts really negatively on their ability to manage resources independently and also adds visual clutter which can affect how the space feels. So the question, 'are we actually doing this to ourselves' crops up!

 What effect does clutter have on children and adults who have limited mobility? Are you taking their physical needs into account?

If you've taken photographs of your learning environment from an adult's and a child's perspective, as part of auditing your space, take a look at them now, noting the amount of resources on offer, visually. How does it make you feel? Very often when we ask delegates to carry out this exercise they are shocked at the way that they have unconsciously become used to the amount of clutter in their environment. We hear stories of cupboards that are so full a serious amount of 'shoving' is needed to get the door closed!

Reviewing the resourcing of a learning environment takes time and care. It's also an emotive process as we are often 'attached' to some equipment, especially if it's been

donated or you've had it for years. One setting had a whole wall length mural painted by a group of parents in bright, garish colours many years ago. The colour scheme and the cartoon characterisation was felt to be inappropriate now, but the team still felt anxious about redecorating, feeling that they were being disloyal and ungrateful.

Another setting shared their anxiety about an outside area that had been constructed as part of a very successful parent partnership project, but this was now not a good use of the space and very few children were engaging with it. Taking it down, felt synonymous with dismantling the project.

As funding streams for services for babies and young children are ever more pressed and reduced we know that we need to increase the shelf life of our current resources, but this in turn can create a temptation to 'hold on' to resources that really are surplus to requirements. This can be challenge for those with decent storage space, but a particular challenge, for those settings who are home based or work in community spaces with little or no dedicated storage areas.

 Could someone stepping into your outside space immediately see the value that you place on children's learning? What is it about this area, the resources and the care that has been demonstrated here that makes your pedagogy clear to all?

Sorting out storage issues and clutter impacts on adults in the space too and contributes to their sense of well-being. Working in light, airy, spacious environments makes people feel more energised and positive, more decisive and creative. It's no surprise that settings where adult space and particularly space for practitioners to access during their breaks is brightened up, tidied, freshly decorated, comfortable and cared for results in a greater sense of energy and motivation.

Misconceptions exist about children instinctively knowing how to make decisions relating to their choice of resources when they are offered in quantity. It is not just the wealth of new resources on offer that can be overwhelming for most children, but the scale of them, both familiar and new. Holding aspirations for our children to be independent decision makers, problem solvers, in charge of their own learning and having high levels of agency is critical, but shelves full of resources

and overflowing boxes of ill-defined items do not help children select what they want or need. Many children may, need help thinking about selecting and choosing, how can they learn how to do this in overwhelming environments?

Another parallel within our adult lives can be helpful here in identifying how selecting from too many resources can be daunting and led to disengagement. At a restaurant with friends you are given the menu to make your choices from. You open the menu to be met with over 25 possible selections for your meal, your heart sinks! You start skimming the descriptions for things you like and those you don't feel like eating today. The waiter hovers ready to take your order, but undecided you ask them to come back in a few minutes. You start using some strategies to help make the decision, asking your friends what their choices are, ruling out some categories, seeing what other people are eating, seeking inspiration from external sources to help you make that all important decision. Again the waiter expectantly appears and this time you feel an obligation to make a decision and so as a deflecting strategy you ask them to start taking orders from the other end of the table and reach you last. As your friends are ordering your resolve to opt for a particular dish changes and waivers dependent on what everyone in the group is having. You make your choice and then another dish catches your eye as it is transported by on a tray, too late you've committed. Your dish arrives and looks ok, but your good friend sat next to you definitely has something more tantalising on their plate!

Do you recognise the scenario? If so, think about how this could have felt, the range of emotions it evoked, tension, indecision, frustration, disappointment, confusion, irritation, overwhelming decisions and dissatisfaction.

Swamping children with 'too much stuff' can feel the same, so it should come as no surprise when we see children flitting between resources, selecting and then moving on, failing to genuinely connect and concentrate.

When resources are visually available at all times, we are in fact not helping children become independent as generally the only people who can competently manage in these conditions are adults. Helping children become aware of what their choices are, but then screening off resources that they are not choosing to engage with can be a very effective way of helping them to choose consciously and engage more deeply. It's not about reducing choice but facilitating developmentally appropriate choice in terms of range and scale. Children still have physical access to resources, but reducing the visual access is helpful. This can easily, cheaply and swiftly be done by covering storage units with light materials for example that can be rolled up and down or drawn to the side to permit access. Choosing a consistent material to do this streamlines the look and feel of the whole space.

Remember that visual distraction is as applicable to over use of text based labelling, extensive displays, patterns and decoration in the learning environment too.

Find out more about visual stress:

www.opticalm.ca
www.irlen.org.uk
www.ceriumoptical.com/vistech/visual-stress.aspx
www.facebook.com/groups/
parentsofkidswithvisualstress/

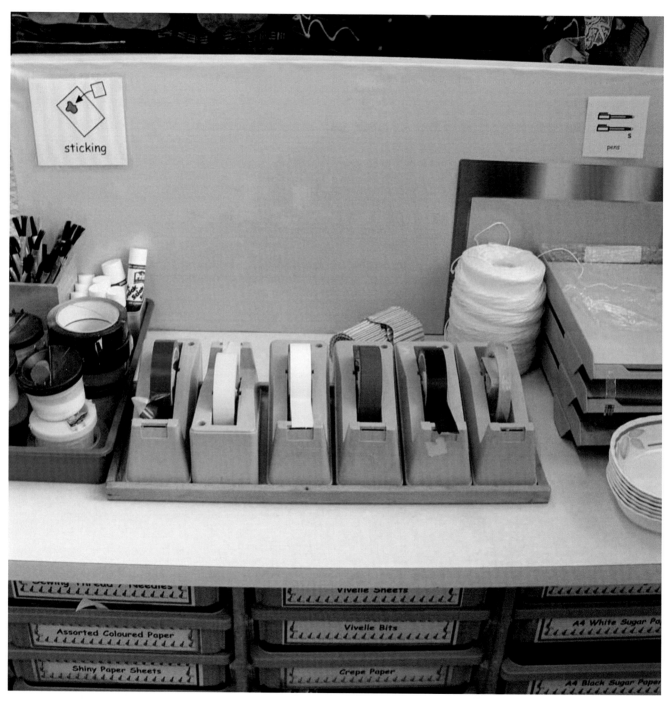

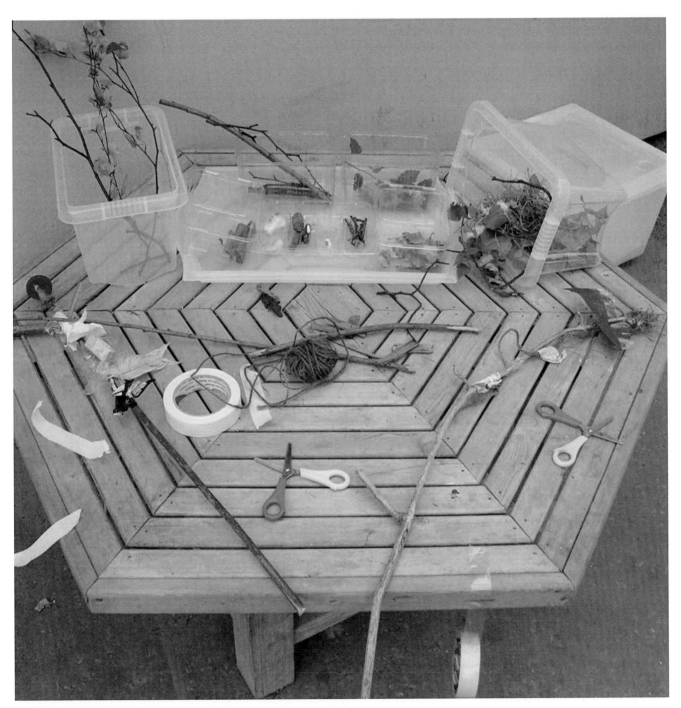

Case Study: Tir-y-Berth Primary School, Wales

"Everything has a place. Work has to be organised," says Debbie, the head.

"Storage helps keep our resources organised. We have custom built storage to hold our storage containers. All of our resources have been sorted into clear boxes, labelled and stored centrally. In classrooms, there are core resources and topic collections linked to the theme they are developing. There is no harbouring allowed. The rest of the resources not being used in classrooms are stored centrally. We have an audit of needs to help us sort out what things to keep or throw.

The team is important...you need the guts to take a risk and courage to throw things out. I've had 25 skips here. We filled them with old things that had been here for years. I now have a skip a term to make sure we don't hold onto unnecessary clutter."

Debbie monitors the classroom environment twice a term for clutter. All support staff have a communal area for the school to keep clutter free. They get fifteen minutes a day to check and keep it tidy.

This helps to reduce the unnecessary influence of distracting resources in the classroom, helping children concentrate on the task at hand, enabling conversations to be focused on what they are trying to achieve rather than delineating off into another conversation about a nearby piece of equipment. It's not about restricting influence but targeting it and encouraging the children to research through speaking and listening.

The advantages of an ordered classroom or space are obvious. Children are able to select what they need from the available and appropriate resources and are not inhibited or restricted by an overwhelming mass of hoarded and possibly irrelevant and outdated materials, which just take up space.

The expansion of space when areas are de-cluttered permits thinking space, space to ponder and consider, such as 'white space' in books and reading materials.

Our brains need time (space) to ingest ideas and mull them over. If you cram every available space with resources, noise and distractions the brain goes into overload. We all know how debilitating that can be. Too much choice can be paralyzing and bring learning to a standstill.

"Storage needs to be considered carefully to offer access. Of course, this is especially relevant to settings who have to set up daily and have no permanent storage facilities. Many of these settings are also restricted by the layout of the room, such as a village hall or home of a childminder, but again some careful thought about the space and the way in which resources are displayed and accessed can have huge implications on learning and social interaction." Ruth Pimentel

What do we actually mean when we use the word 'resource'?

Working with the CFS™ Approach has given us much to think about. When we explore the resource offer of most settings we ask practitioners some key questions and they always include the following:

- What is the purpose of this resource?
- What meaning does this resource have for each child?
- How does it add to concrete learning experiences?
- How does that resource make connections for children?
- Why did you select it?
- How are children interacting with it?
- How do you extend and vary its use and appeal?
- What would happen if you didn't have it?
- Do you enjoy using it?

If you'd struggle answering any of these questions about your resources, that should tell you something about the benefits that they are or are not bringing to your learning environment.

Thankfully, we are seeing an ever increasing shift away from plastic dominated resource offers to a more balanced selection, featuring more collections of natural, tactile, open ended resources.

We fundamentally know that the more a toy does the less a child does. When we see children unable to make something from 'nothing', that should ring alarm bells to us that we are not providing them with resources that tap into their creativity. Sadly for some children, their ability to free up their creativity is hampered because they have too much, or just 'pre-determined toys'. We need resources that help children wonder 'what if', triggered by the resources available to them. Less can definitely be more. This is of course where the quality issue comes in- quality is an ambiguous word, what represents quality to one, does not to another.

What we are looking for is not a singularly quality resource, but the prompts and triggers for quality play. This can only be done by matching our resource offer with observations of children's current fascinations and interests.

It is also about having developmentally appropriate resources for the children that you are working with today, not a resource offer that is always based on traditional thinking (ie we are 'expected' to have this), but an aligned, responsive offer.

Having a solid understanding of child development is at the core of getting your resource offer right. Acknowledging stages of play- the child who can only cope with short bursts of parallel play but reverts to a more comfortable solitary play stage for a time, will have a developmental need for a certain selection of items to support this; only having resources that require consistent engagement with others will not work. Likewise, tuning into schema's in children's play will enable a more relevant set of resources (natural and artificial, recycled and bought, familiar and regular) to be shared that will enhance and scaffold learning expertly.

If your children are not engaging with your resources, perhaps it's not down to them, perhaps your selection is mismatched to their developmental stage and current interests/ learning preferences.

Are you inspired by your resources?

Resources made from natural materials have a greater appeal to all the learning senses, including smell, which can often be overlooked. Multi-sensory resources are undoubtedly more interesting to interact with. Very often they are free or available for only a token cost and when selected sensitively and respectfully from nature can be plentiful, seasonal, replaced easily and help children connect with the natural world. Look out for opportunities within a recycling and repurposing context too. Stores that have closing down sales, charity shops, friends who are moving home and Scrapstores (local companies that donate excess materials to support education), and donation websites, are all great places to look for recycled resources. Remember however, to control your tendencies to over clutter and only collect what you are genuinely going to use!

Resourcing learning environments to reflect the child's home context is essential. This must be done respectfully and with resources and artefacts that are familiar, able to be handled freely and make sense to the children. Asking parents/carers for information and donations of items that they have finished with is a great way of ensuring that practitioner knowledge is relevant and resources sourced appropriately. Families enjoy sharing their heritage with you and making connections between their home and their children's setting.

Resourcing a learning environment tends to build up over time as funds become available and additional items are sought. Try if you can to keep an overview on what you have and how it all links together. If you simply keep adding to your existing quantity and don't consciously think about instigating a trading policy such as 'one in one out' the volume will build up over time without you noticing. Also be careful about making rash decisions when faced with a 'bargain' or a time pressured decision on using funds by a deadline- these are both sure fire ways of inappropriately making decisions about resourcing.

 Resources need interested adults too. Each time you interact with a resource you send out a subtle message about what you think about it. We set the scene for learning and must model genuine fascination and intrigue. When was the last time your children saw you engrossed?

When looking at how children use resources it's also important to notice where they take them to. Observe whether they use things differently in different places. We've noticed this is particularly useful when areas that have been intentionally set up do not produce the expected (adult) outcomes. For example 'writing areas' restricted to hard tables and chairs in busy thoroughfares may not light up children's interest in their emerging skills, but the same resources transported to a garden den space might be central to the play and give the basis of a wonderfully accomplished skills observation for example.

Access to resources can also be limited or even completely wiped out by poor presentation, or for example, by displaying resources in ways that prevent clear visual presentation. Try to use plain cloths, backing or storage methods so that the shape, texture and colours of the items are easily definable from any background, to make presentation more visually inclusive and inviting.

Find out More

Less is More Checklist: Classroom Spaces that Work, Clayton and Forton, In the Issue, Spring 2001, Vol 13, No 2

Atelier: Furnishings for young children ISBN 88-87960-14-3 available in Italian and English

Play and Soft: Suggested furnishings from international research project. ISBN 88-87960-41-0 available in Italian and English

Threads of Thinking: Schemas and Young Children's Learning. In her new edition of this popular book, Cathy Nutbrown presents evidence of continuity and progression in young children's thinking. She shows, with detailed observation, that they are able and active learners. She considers aspects of children's patterns of learning and thinking - or schemas - and demonstrates clearly how children learn in an active, dynamic and creative way. ISBN 978-1849204644

e and Cassius share the transient art materials.

Alfie places the be one at a time.

Ellie carefully positions the berries with her fingers.

Orla places bunches of berries in the nut shells.

Joshua carefully arranges the stones on the wood blocks.

Sharing Children's Work and Display

All too often, the environment is planned by adults for adults, yet we know that the space belongs to and is for children. Sometimes adults can become more concerned about the opinions of other adults and what they think about the setting. This routine error can lead to a crucial lack of focus and confidence regarding what is right for children.

If we roll the clock back many years, it was traditional for adults to 'manage' children's 'artwork' for display. Once complete, adults took's great pride in displaying work as perfectly as possible, often with the display board covered in highly patterned and coloured paper which actually distracted from the children's work. This might have been complemented by things hanging from the ceiling and on washing lines across the room. The result was often poorly defined children's work, displayed too high up for children to interact with and all too busy. As with all progressive practice, this approach is now diminishing and we are seeing children's work in all its original glory come to the fore, displayed with sensitivity and respect and with a greater emphasis on process or learning, not always a product.

"There is a special speech and language room where children have specialist input. This room is deliberately barer than the rest of the school. Displays are kept simple. There are quiet work spaces. The bottom part of window overlooking an internal corridor has been blocked out to prevent children being distracted by other children walking by." Tir-Y-Berth Primary School, Wales.

Displays work best when they add to the impact that the learning environment makes. In order to create a more streamlined look it may be helpful to use one consistent colour as backing for the children's work - which after all, is often what the display is for. Calm, natural colours, hessian and cardboard all make stunning yet subtle backgrounds. Think about an art gallery where generally the display space has been created to guide your eye to the pieces of work which are the focal point of the exhibition or display. In that way, your experience as a viewer is a good one; you can concentrate and explore, focus and not become distracted by the extraneous clutter on the walls, floors and window space.

We've worked in early years settings and schools to help teachers and practitioners think about the impact of cramming every available piece of wall, ceiling, floor and window space with images, text and artefacts. Many have told us that they have taken this approach because it was 'what was expected of them and how they felt they were judged by colleagues, families and visitors'. When they asked their children what was on display and whether they referred to the textual prompts they found that in most cases the children couldn't recall what was up on the walls, things had often been there for so long that the display had become like wallpaper. Children also mentioned that they often didn't read the textual prompts because they were too far away to read comfortably and were distorted. Reflecting on this, teachers and practitioners have radically overhauled the way that they use display, wall coverings, carpets and artefacts hanging from ceilings and left windows clear to create opportunities for more natural light.

By Brad Willis

By Jessica Howard

By Kayla Charles Asman

The Effects of Noise

"Everything in writing begins with language. Language begins with listening." Jeanette Winterson, Writer

 Is your learning environment 'listening friendly?'

Over the past 30 years, there have been many research studies into the links between children's noise exposure and their performance in school. Research at the start of the 1990's concluded that chronic noise exposure in young children had particularly detrimental effects on reading ability. More recently, Picard and Bradley[1] have published a major review of issues related to speech intelligibility in classrooms, which covers many aspects of noise and acoustics in the classroom.

The assumption that children, equates to noise is stereotypical and can lead to an assumption that noise levels are bound to be high and so we do nothing to reduce them.

"The general effects of chronic noise exposure on children are deficits in sustained attention and visual attention; poorer auditory discrimination and speech perception; poorer memory for tasks that require the high processing demands of semantic material; and poorer reading ability and school performance based on national standardised tests." Shield and Dockrell

Our physical space can contribute significantly to noise levels, particularly those which have a lot of hard surfaces, which act as a trampoline for noise making it 'bounce' around the space, echoing and amplifying; another good reason to think about softening some of your space with sound absorbing equipment and resources such as more soft furnishings, rugs, material on display boards and lowering ceilings with drapes.

Becoming distracted by noise can also be an issue, particularly those noise sources that we cannot do very much about. Here again, it's worth thinking about positioning of equipment and layout. For example, turning the entrance to a story sharing area around to face a wall instead of looking out into the room, which could be full of visual and auditory distraction. This can reduce visual and auditory distraction experienced by children and adults in a space that needs relative quiet to be effective and enjoyed.

Listening as a skill takes a while to develop. Babies and very young children are less able to be multi-focused and so planning their learning environments needs special attention to ensure that activities which require such a high level cognitive skill as listening are offered in an appropriate context, ie a listening friendly one. This might mean that a focus on access to that space, routine, the interruptions of other adults and extraneous noise from equipment that can be temporarily silenced takes place to set the scene for optimum results. Don't be tempted to apologise to other adults for asking them to 'tone it down'. Secure pedagogy means that everyone understands the importance of speaking and listening.

When reviewing your whole layout, notice what activities are adjacent to others. Occasionally we have seen inadvertently placed opposing activities too close to each other and whilst making noise is of course very valid, if it is next to a space where we'd like children to be able to hear the clarity of speech sounds for example, it can have a detrimental effect.

[1] Picard and Bradley 2001 Revisiting speech interference in classrooms

Be very aware of children with limited mobility and those with hearing deficits. Make yourself knowledgeable about hearing impairment, things like:

- What it feels like to wear a hearing aid which amplifies all sounds not just human voices
- Using visual clues to aid communication
- Difficulties in screening out background sounds and 'white noise'
- Children who suffer with inconsistent hearing conditions and how this affects them on a daily basis
- Being in front of children before you start to speak
- The value of gentle touch in alerting and redirecting attention
- Working with parents'/carers to learn and understand together

Just as it's helpful to know where your talking hotspots are in your learning environment- places where talk happens most regularly, it's also helpful to know where your quiet hotspots are too and make use of them to support listening.

You may also need to think beyond your immediate space. What's happening directly outside, in the corridor, in the room next door or upstairs? The impact of noisy neighbours can be as apparent in schools and settings as it can at home. Becoming aware of particularly noisy times or activities might indicate that a change in routines, positioning of activities or a joint planning session might enable you to identify times when this is more likely to create a difficulty and make some provision to minimise the negative implications.

Many children are extremely sensitive to noise and this can make them anxious when spending time in environments that are busy, frantic and loud. You may know a child who is reluctant to be in areas which are noisy and busy. It can be helpful to create some quiet, calm spaces both inside and outside for children to use to make the transition from one area to another and where they can spend time in spaces where the volume level suits their individual preferences. Monitor the specific times during the day when the noise levels rise. For example, does lunchtime seem a particularly noisy time? Why? Does the layout of the furniture, the mix of children or adults and children make any difference? How could these issues be overcome or a least minimised?

"Listening is a magnetic and strange thing, a creative force. The friends who listen to us are the ones we move toward. When we are listened to, it creates us, makes us unfold and expand." Karl Menninger, Psychiatrist

Did you know that even back in 1958 this was a problem! Have things improved today?

"Classrooms may be noisy…simply because of the way they are constructed and finished. It is a shocking fault, for the need to hear well is basic in education."McQuade, Schoolhouse, 1958.

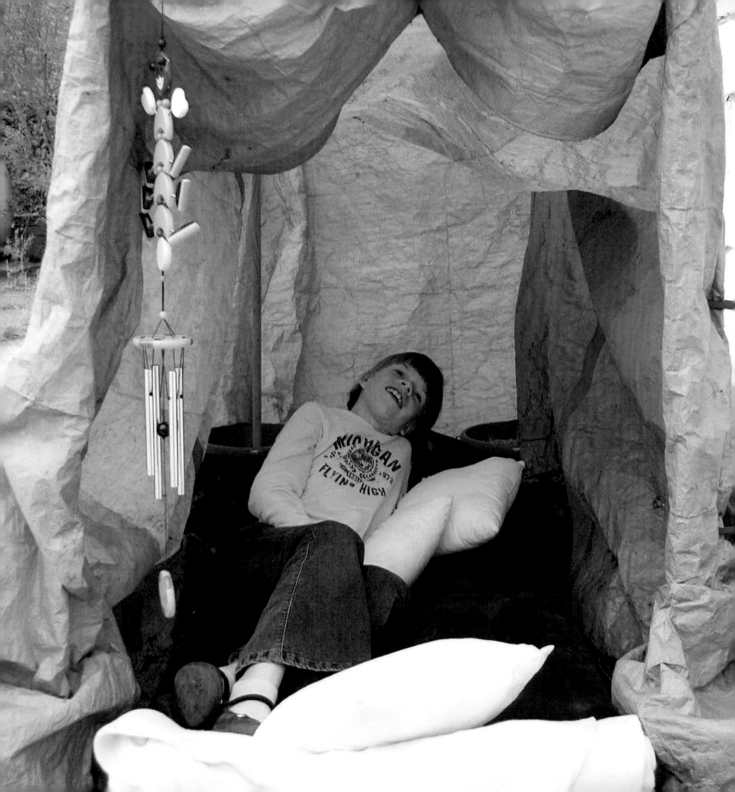

Don't forget that watching is an important part of listening. When we listen we are observing and interpreting more than the sounds available to us and so good visibility is also a determining factor.

Are your communication skills worth copying? If the children that you work with replicated your exact communication skill set what would we see? Be worthy of duplicating.

Remember some of these simple communication basics:

- Don't interrupt, wait for people to finish what they have to say.
- Focus on what is being said, not half listening waiting for a pause so that you can speak.
- It's not a competition! You don't always have to pitch in with your own version of the topic.
- Give your full, present attention to the person who is speaking.
- Use your non-verbal communication skills in ways that are congruous with your verbal skills (ie no mixed messages).
- Use pauses and give yourself time to process and think.
- Use people's names to indicate their value and your shared connection.

 You can help to inform and support parents/ carers to identify how they too can encourage speaking and listening skills through the environment they create for their child at home.

For example, the influence of unconnected noises such as a television, or radio and the impact that this can have on the child's ability to listen and hold a conversation.

Are your colleagues aware of just how much noise and distraction they create? Sit and listen for a while and acknowledge what are the components of noise in your learning environment, what could be changed to improve this? Who might you need to speak to?

On occasions it may be that other adults in your school or setting are creating noise through their conversations. This might be a sensitive issue to raise but awareness of the impact of your actions is vital. Taking a whole school/setting approach to noise awareness can be extremely helpful to everyone.

What else contributes to excessive noise in your learning environment?

Find out more

Noise In Learning Environments: ELIZABETH JARMAN®
Foundation. www.elizabethjarmanfoundation.org.uk

www.quietclassrooms.org gives research examples and
guidance on controlling noise pollution in schools and
public places

www.uea.ac.uk for information on the Birmingham study

www.hounslow.gov.uk for information on the aircraft noise
pollution feedback

The Effects of Noise on Children at School: A Review
Bridget M Shield and Julie E Dockrell For more detail on
sources of noise, effects of environmental noise, effects
of classroom noise, children's perceptions of noise at
school, noise levels and acoustic classroom standards

Stephen Pretlove, Reader in Architectural Science and
Technology, Kingston University, has researched building
acoustics. The faculty's 'ArchiLab' carries out assessments
of noise levels both inside and outside buildings and
makles 'noise maps' for public areas available for
public information. http://www.kingston.ac.uk/news/
findanexpert/profile/193/Stephen-Pretlove/

The Targeted Use of Colour

Colour is commonly associated with 'psychological temperature'. It can have a huge impact on our response both physically and emotionally. Historically children's spaces have involved colour and lots of it, mostly from the primary colour pallete. However, it's worth thinking about why our own homes are not decorated in the same way that we might choose for a learning environment. When we ask delegates on training this question they are typically shocked and refuse our offer of a free makeover of their home using only bold, bright, primary colours! 'Why not?' we ask, 'No way' we are told 'I couldn't live with that; I need somewhere calm to relax and enjoy my space'.

When we wonder why masses of bold, bright, primary colours have historically been used we can find no convincing evidence to support it. People perhaps associated those colours with fun and associate fun with children. You only need to look at some of your local community venues or children's play areas or waiting zones for families in airports for example to see what we mean. Of course, learning needs to have a healthy dose of fun and colour, but growing brains is a serious business and the context and environment within which they are evolving deserves more consideration now we understand so much more about its impact and the way that the use of colour can be targeted.

Research indicates that when deciding which colours you should use in a learning environment it's really important to consider the purpose of the space. Colours need to be chosen carefully and with consideration of the layout for the room, position of windows and sun-exposure.

The following basic guidelines, dating back to the '60's when Dr. Max Luscher created his colour test. Read through and then think about how you use colour.

Colour and responses:

Blue - Feels tranquil, cool, serene: certain shades of blue cause the brain to secrete tranquillising chemicals and can be perceived as cold.

Green - Makes people feel secure and 'tended', persistent and self-centred, can be dull.

Red - Increases respiratory rates, stimulates eating, can increase blood pressure, feels exciting and invites impulsiveness: over-exposure can result in agitation.

Yellow - Recognised by humans faster than any other colour, evokes spontaneity, is joyful, optimistic, warm and signifies communication!

Orange - Dominant, lively: peachy orange is warm, bright orange is non-relaxing.

Terracotta/Brown - Evokes 'back to earth' feelings.

Violet - Can be overpowering, pastels are better for background.

Kaleidoscope Project, Pepper Hill First School, Milton Keynes:

In this project children joined in colour and light therapy sessions. Evidence indicated that they become calmer and more self-confident, more ready to learn. The Kaleidoscope Project proved so effective, a wider roll out was suggested. School absence was down by 33% and SATs results improved by a third.

Visual Inclusion

For children and adults who have a variety of visual difficulties, highly patterned equipment can be more difficult to use and enjoy and in some cases makes visual discrimination between 2 and 3D much more challenging. The use of highly patterned tablecloths for instance, can contribute to a lack of edge definition.

Ideally the main decorative theme in a learning environment should be consistent, using a single colour in varying shades, or a harmonious complementary scheme using colours which do not clash and are selected from a natural palette. In schools and settings where this has been carried out teachers and practitioners have observed children who are a lot calmer and therefore more able to concentrate and interestingly adults have indicated that they feel calmer too. This has had a positive effect on practice and the children's response.

It's about using colour in an informed, manageable way. A lack of colour would be detrimental too. We need colour in our lives. Being brave enough to take on a colour review as part of adopting the CFS™ Approach can be one of the most challenging and trigger the greatest response from colleagues and families.

When we've have caught up with delegates who have reviewed the use of colour in their environments, they tell us that they have often had to overcome critics and doubters, telling them that the learning environment no longer looks 'fun or for children'. However, once they then go on to share examples of the children becoming calmer, more engaged, spending longer in complex play activities and a noted increase in their communication skills their understanding is enhanced and those positive commentaries help to illustrate the positive impact of the CFS™ approach in practice.

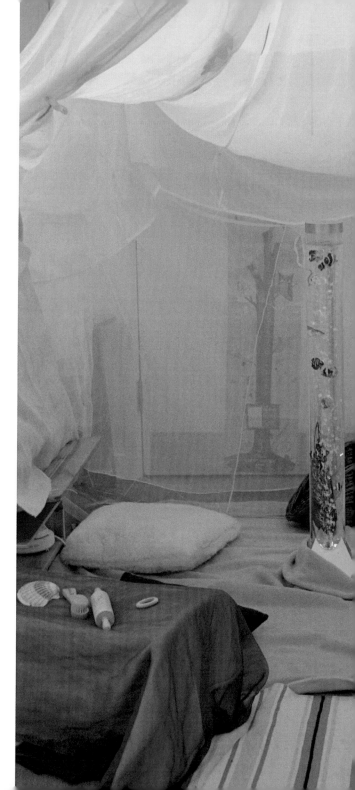

- *Deep, 'warm' colours give learning spaces an intimate, cosy feeling*
- *Light, 'cool' colours make a classroom seem more spacious and have a calming effect*
- *Wall colours can be warm or cool tones, but keep the colours fairly light and not greyed*
- *It is a mistake to 'go overboard' with lots of bright, primary colours. This is just as bad as an all black and white room*
- *Clean, clear, light colours are usually best for a learning atmosphere (www.glidden.com)*

(Taken from Barbara Prashnig's article Colour Me Beautiful, Education TODAY Issue 6, 2004).

- *Is your environment sensitive to the way that colour is used?*
- *What is the strongest feature in your learning environment- does the colour take over? Are you and the children coping with a colour explosion?*
- *How could your learning spaces be supported by targeted and more manageable use of colour?*
- *What colours would optimise learning in your setting?*
- *How does colour affect you? Do you respond to varying depths, shades and mixes of colour?*
- *Imagine yourself as a child wanting to spend time with a friend looking at a book together - what is your vision of the ideal space? What colours feel right?*

Find out more

Colour and Light. Dr. Max Luscher's colour test: http://www.colourtest.ue-foundation.org/

For more information about suitable colours for classroom settings: www.glidden.com

For more information about style, diversity, colours and lighting in classrooms see www.creativelearningcentre.com

For further and recent research visit www.surfaceandmedia.blogspot.com to find out about Anke Jakob's post doctoral research at the Design research Centre, Kingston University. This work considers the calming effect of using restricted colour palettes and the impact on well being.

www.colour.org.uk is the website for a colour group formed in the 1940s to explore the effect of colour on people and society.

The CFS™ Approach and the targeted use of colour in learning environments: The ELIZABETH JARMAN® Magazine Issue 7, 2013.

Available at www.elizabethjarmantraining.co.uk or on iTunes.

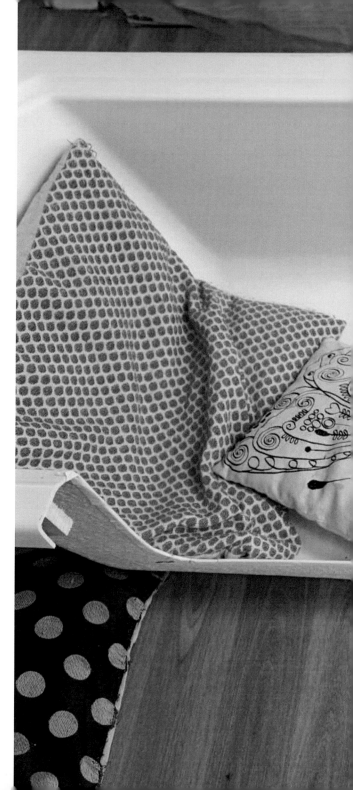

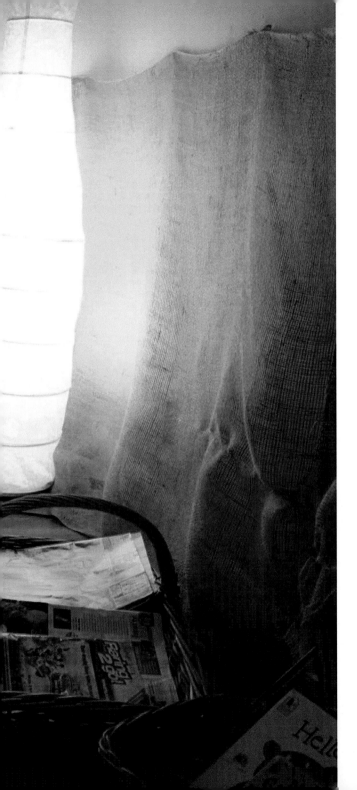

The Impact of Light

We are all energised by natural sunlight. It makes us feel more energized, more creative and more 'switched on'. Day lighting studies provide convincing evidence that children progress more quickly in naturally lit environments. We need to consider how to maximise natural light in our learning environments to create optimum conditions for learning.

Students with lots of daylight in their classrooms progressed 20% faster in maths and 26% faster in reading in one year than those with the least
www.pge.com

There can be a feeling that light is one of the things in an environment, that we have least control or influence over. It's true that in many learning environments the artificial lights only have the on or off option! However, if, as soon as we enter the space each morning we put the lights on automatically we need to stop right there and consider if we really need them and what type of 'mood' or light level we are attempting to create. Generally at home we are quite expert at creating mood with our domestic lights, using lamps, curtains, blinds, spotlights, dimmers and natural daylight to enhance whatever activity we are involved in. We do instinctively know what works for us regarding light levels.

As one teacher commented recently "I've just realised I prefer to read when I am laid down somewhere soft such as a sofa and have a small lamp on. No wonder my children don't feel comfortable sitting on hard chairs at tables under harsh artificial lighting!"

Natural sunlight provides the bonus of vitamin D, hopefully a little safe warmth and as long as it's not too glaring. Light can be a magical resource.

Notice how light moves around a room with the passing of the sun throughout the day and if it causes glare and high penetrating heat; as this is particularly important for non- mobile babies and those children with limited or no independent mobility. Just as adults, children are sensitive to variance of light.

Don't cover every available space around windows with displays, or curtains which then block the source of light. This is relevant in every setting and a simple action to take to improve the learning environment for children. Place resources and equipment in areas that receive a lot of natural light to aid discovery and investigation. Move furniture from positions that block the light coming in.

Muted light can be relaxing, cosy and safe, enabling children to settle into speaking and listening activities in a comfortable space which encourages them to stay engaged. Use drapes, blinds and nets to diffuse light or to add a change of hue to the light in your environment.

We can also consider using artificial lights to create mood and atmosphere. Light boxes can offer a range of different physical conditions at a switch and subsequently affect the environment. This could be used to zone activities such as colour indicating quiet areas for chatting, sharing books and stories.

Using safe, flexible lighting, give children some control about deciding how much light they prefer. They very rarely have the opportunity to control the light levels where they spend their time as usually the light levels have been selected by someone else.

Methwold Nursery in Thetford, Norfolk

Owner Janet Lamport and Nursery manager Fiona Penny took photographs of their nursery and started a serious de-clutter! They noted there were so many toys in the space and have now really adopted a 'less is more' approach. In December they closed for one week, painted the walls and created a draped cosy area in main room.

They made sure that the storage boxes in each area were only one colour i.e. not red and yellow and their long term plan is to purchase clear containers or baskets. They already benefit from wood laminate flooring and wooden storage units. In one area they turned the drawers round to hide the bright colours on the front. They revamped the notice board for parents which had a 'loud' coloured background and used cork boards instead.

Really noticeable changes happened when they focused on the lighting and purchased a number of plain uplighters. These have had a dramatic effect and created a lovely soft and calming light. Children are also encouraged to take their shoes off indoors to quieten the noise levels. Parents have commented on the difference and the word is out and more parents asking to bring their children to the nursery!

They have noted how much the children's behaviour has altered from these changes onwards- they are much more relaxed, especially four children designated as having Special Educational Needs. This positive change is particularly marked on Mondays when children come in after a busy weekend at home!

Janet also felt staff were much calmer and concluded that CFS™ is having a positive effect on everyone.

Find out more

Jack Mama, Creative Director of Probes Programme, Philips Design, www.design.philips.com/probes asks., 'What do we need a particular lighting for?' His work explores the idea of ambient effects versus task lighting, and the use of emotional sensing in light sources.

Hungarian architect, Aron Losonczi has researched the notion of illuminated wall claddings and light-transmitting concrete, both of which could be used in educational settings. www.litracon.hu

Martin Richman (www.martinrichman.com) has completed commissions for schools and his work focuses on colour and light. He is inspired by growing up on a beach and talks about 'boundless space and limitless possibilities'. His interests lie in exploring different cultural reactions and attitudes to colour and light

www.guardian.co.uk/teacher-network/2013/apr/25/changing-classroom-environment-improve-learning

Sharing the CFS™ Approach with Families

Sharing this thinking with families is important. Just as we've explored the advantages of listening to children, working collaboratively with families is essential when we are making changes to a learning environment so that we can build a holistic picture of the sorts of places where children are most confidently communicating, to feed into planning. It will also help families to understand why the learning environment is set up in a certain way and what simple changes they could perhaps make at home to enhance communication skills there.

Conclusions

Throughout this guidance we have merged some of the early thinking about CFS™ with more recent evidence about this approach as our understanding is still evolving. The principles underpinning the approach have been used in a wide range of contexts. How will they help to improve the environment where you work? Here are some key points to reflect on:

- The development of communication and language is at the heart of children's learning.
- A communication friendly environment is the key to improving speaking and listening.
- The environment must align with the pedagogy of the school or setting. It must be overt and clear to all stakeholders.
- Re-thinking embedded concepts is difficult, but not impossible.
- Space comes in all shapes and sizes and is both indoor and outdoor.
- We are responsible for the layout of our settings and schools and we can change it!
- Children are naturally sociable, but also like to have space to withdraw to and work in small groups or alone.
- Over-stimulation is not helpful and can be detrimental to learning.
- Space needs to be inviting for children to use and may need to be modelled to give them ideas about welcome behaviours there.
- The considered use of colour, light, acoustics and materials is crucial to the development of speaking and listening.
- Improvements and changes do not have to cost any money.
- De-cluttering does not have to mean throwing away!
- A cluttered environment clutters learning.
- Too much choice can be paralysing.
- Teachers and practitioners are affected as much as the children by the environment that they work in.
- The contribution that families make is crucial.

Once there was
who, one day, fou
stuck on the moor
and he was not a

Next steps

We recognise that this piece of work presents challenges to established thinking and practice.

We are very keen to receive feedback about how you use the CFS™ Approach wherever you work and the impact it has on speaking and listening skills, emotional well-being, physical development and general engagement.

Why not use the CFS™ audit tool on the following pages to assist you in reviewing your environment, to inform change?

Stay updated with new research, case studies and project reports via our bi-monthly ELIZABETH JARMAN® Magazine. It's available in both hard copy and digitally.

See www.elizabethjarmantraining.co.uk for more details.

The Communication Friendly Spaces™ Approach Audit Tool

This document is intended to serve as a prompt for critical thinking and professional review when considering the implications and opportunities of creating a developmentally appropriate learning environment.

Its aim is to give you confidence in acknowledging that sometimes the stereotype that a learning environment may not be a developmentally appropriate one and to encourage you, and your team if you work as part of one, to step back from your existing viewpoint and consider ways in which informed change might align more closely with the current needs and fascinations of your children.

The prompts and suggestions have been generated by best practice examples that we have observed and discussed with practitioners and families; everyone's view is helpful in guiding us to create an environment that genuinely suits those using the space.

The principles of the Communication Friendly Spaces™ Approach are woven through it to support thinking.

Where is the best place to start?

In order to consider new thinking we have to be prepared to challenge existing ideas. This can be uncomfortable as we prepare to shed some (certainly not all) of the things that we have always done and remember that some people prefer the safety of the current status quo rather than a new vision, despite this being an opportunity for professional growth.

Reflecting on the areas of discussion and shared imagery contained in this handbook, are there aspects of your practice and environment that you need to think about challenging and questioning?

Capture them here:

Pedagogy for All

Clarity around your pedagogical commitments in relation to a learning environment is at the core of any developments that you decide to take forward. This should be explicit and evident to everyone who accesses your services. Being able to articulate this is essential. Jargon free!

Consult with relevant people to gain perspectives on what matters here. Remember to think about the support strategies that some families might require or seek.

How does your social pedagogy include vital work with families?

Commit in writing- 'What do you want for your children and their families?'

Your influence and impact. Auditing your practice

Having clarified your pedagogical aspirations for your children and their families it's important to acknowledge your impact as expert practitioners in their lives; genuine, caring, warm and knowledgeable adults can offer that necessary emotional support for parents/carers, to build confidence in their role as primary carers.

Here are some questions and prompts regarding your practice, designed to complement your current thinking:

- How are families informed about your setting and what it offers? Is information presented in ways that are clear, helpful and inclusive? Is it only presented in a written format?
- What efforts do you make to meet all prospective families and share your setting and its opportunities with them?
- How do you support families who are using services for the first time? How might that feel for them?
- What professional language do you use? Do you occasionally slip into jargon?
- Is your policy on settling in flexible enough to respond to families' individual needs? How do you share your approach in ways that make this clear and non-judgemental?
- How aware of attachment theory and practice are you? Do you need to revisit this?
- How confident in your knowledge are you of child development? Are your expectations always appropriate given the unique child's context?
- Parents/carers must feel intrinsic to their child's development and achievement, how do you explain this to them at the start of your relationship and throughout their time with you?
- Have you thought about how you are going to share developmental information with families in line with your country's recommendations?
- What is the quality of role modelling taking place? Are your actions and words worth copying?

- Could your expertise be inadvertently 'distancing'? How can you practice in an 'alongside' way?
- Do you share how children have experienced your environment and learning- not just the 'Wow' moments but the everyday occurrences too?
- How could you include appropriate references about the characteristics of effective teaching and learning within those conversations/updates?
- Do you (and your colleagues if you have them) view yourselves as 'enablers, playful and conversation partners' in children's lives? Is your 'engagement' evident?
- Do you (and your colleagues if you have them) view yourselves as supporting 'whole' families?
- Do you have a good idea of things, times of day, certain situations that your families might find more stressful than others? What have you done/could you do to minimise the stress?
- How can you share strategies for coping in respectful, non-judgemental ways?
- Do you ensure that at least once every day you comment on something to somebody that lifts them? Do you know why this has such a positive impact?
- Do you have strategies in place to support practitioners?

Record notes relating to the questions and respond to the following statement:

After reviewing my/our current practitioner impact and influence I/we think that this aspect could be even better if…

After reviewing my/our current practitioner impact and influence I/we think that this aspect could be even better if…

Your physical space. Auditing your learning environment.

Your physical learning environment, inside and outside, should demonstrate your pedagogy in a practical way. For many of our children and their families, the learning environment should be a place of possibility, an emotionally secure space, full of focus and developmentally appropriate early intervention.

Again, here are a range of questions and prompts; this time considering your physical space and resourcing to stimulate your professional awareness of this contributing factor to best practice:

- Have you recently walked around your space imagining that you are new here?
- How does it feel to arrive at your setting? What aspects are welcoming and what might send out mixed messages?
- What recent transitions have you personally made-what parallels can you make with the transitional process your children make?
- What does inclusion mean to you and how is this indicated non-verbally in your space as well as in text or image formats?
- Do you have places for families to sit comfortably, to talk together, to talk with you and linger, is your space participation friendly?
- Have you taken photographs from an adult and a child's height so that you can appreciate how your space looks to all users? What might this tell you?
- How are your children organised? If it's practicable, could you take advantage of the natural mentoring and peer support offered by family grouping?
- Are there places for children (and perhaps adults too) who spend some of their time as observers, to watch from, supporting their personal, social and emotional development?
- Does your space include connections for children and families? Photos and other ways of representing things that matter to them and they are familiar?

- Are there familiar and unfamiliar items and resources in your learning environment? Things that are a pleasure to discover?
- Is the scale of resourcing genuinely in line with developmental expectations for your chil-dren across the age range that you cater for? Are they overwhelmed and facing sensory over load with the amount of choice? Do they know how to choose and select what they want?
- Is your learning environment organised and user responsive?
- Do you have some areas that have no predefined function indicating that anything is pos-sible there?
- Is a proportion of your environment unencumbered with space to move, create, settle and select?
- What does the size and scale of your space, indoors and outside feel like for all of your children?
- How does appropriate risk assessment aligned with the requirements of any relevant legislation sit alongside enabling your children to learn about and manage risk? What are your limits? How do parents/carers feel about 'risk' in this context?
- Are your children getting their recommended minutes of physical activity per day? How does your environment promote this?
- Is it possible for children to learn about and develop skills of independence in your learning environment?
- How much nurturing softness is in your environment-inside and out? Could this be increased?
- Can the children access equipment and resources in different ways and move them around your space? What are your thoughts about children moving equipment and resources?
- Are there visual and text indicators that give hints about how resources might be used? Is there informative and useful signage shared in inclusive ways, but not excessive?
- Do you have duplicates or multiples of favoured resources and books, enabling increased

engagement and reducing the behavioural implications of 24/7 sharing (tricky at any age!)?

- Do you enjoy spending a large proportion of your week in your learning environment?
- What are the noise levels like in your space? Does it have any impact?
- Are there small spaces, proportionate to children's need for calmness, opportunities for intended withdrawal, privacy, self-regulation and recharging?
- How does your space flow?
- Can children access outside and inside in line with their preferences? Do you know their preferences and how do you share these observations and suggestions with families?
- Do you have small collections of natural, open ended resources that can be combined?
- How do you link schematic play observations to your resource offer?
- Are your resources truly diverse?
- Would you describe your resources as quality?
- Can your children handle real life and 'real' resources rather than just toy replicas?
- How can your children use your resources to replicate the adult activities they've observed, such as mark making, communicating, and real life experiences, especially if they do not yet have verbal language to utilise?
- What is the proportion of natural to man-made resources in your learning environment?
- How does your resource offer link explicitly to your observations of your children and their interests and play preferences?
- Is 'time' as a key resource fully appreciated?
- How are abstract experiences represented in a concrete way?
- Do you offer resources and activities at different heights? (kneeling, low level, stood up, on the move etc)
- What spaces and resources facilitate calm behaviours and stillness as developmentally appropriate?
- What could you do to enhance your learning environment at no cost, by recycling and repurposing?
- What gaps have you identified? What are you going to do about them?

Of course, this list is not exhaustive but should give you a flavour of some of the things to consider regarding the physical space for your children.

Capture your responses to the questions on the following pages and again visualise and respond to the following:

After reviewing my/our physical learning environment I/we think that it could be even better if…

After reviewing my/our physical learning environment I/we think that it could be even better if...

You might want to link this audit with other quality framework documents that you are currently using to continually review. Add in relevant images and observations to validate and evidence your thinking and progression.

ELIZABETH JARMAN® Publications

A PLACE TO TALK
FOR TWO YEAR OLDS
One in a series of books to support language development in young children
Elizabeth Jarman

A PLACE TO TALK
FOR BABIES
One in a series of books to support language development in young children
Elizabeth Jarman

A PLACE TO TALK
AT HOME
One in a series of books to support language development in young children
Elizabeth Jarman

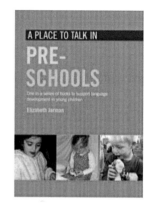

A PLACE TO TALK IN
PRE-SCHOOLS
One in a series of books to support language development in young children
Elizabeth Jarman

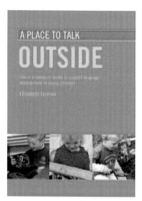

A PLACE TO TALK
OUTSIDE
One in a series of books to support language development in young children
Elizabeth Jarman

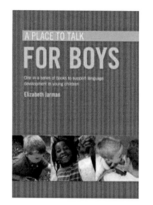

A PLACE TO TALK
FOR BOYS
One in a series of books to support language development in young children
Elizabeth Jarman

A PLACE TO TALK IN
PACK-AWAY SETTINGS
One in a series of books to support language development in young children
Elizabeth Jarman

A PLACE TO TALK IN
CHILDREN'S CENTRES
One in a series of books to support language development in young children
Elizabeth Jarman

A PLACE TO TALK
IN KS1
One in a series of books to support language development in young children
Elizabeth Jarman

A PLACE TO TALK
AT MY CHILD-MINDER'S
One in a series of books to support language development in young children
Elizabeth Jarman

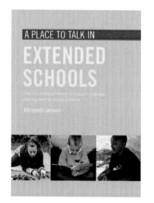

A PLACE TO TALK IN
EXTENDED SCHOOLS
One in a series of books to support language development in young children
Elizabeth Jarman

ELIZABETH JARMAN®
THE COMMUNICATION FRIENDLY SPACES APPROACH

CFS™ SPECIAL EDITION
THE CFS™ APPROACH SUPPORTING PHYSICAL DEVELOPMENT
ELIZABETH JARMAN

Useful related reading

- McGrath,H and Francey, S '91. Friendly Kids Friendly Classrooms-Teaching Social Skills and Confidence in the Classroom, Longman Cheshire, Melbourne (The Friendly Kids Friendly Classrooms Social Skills Programme, Australia)
- School Design Impacts upon Cognitive Learning: Defining "Equal Educational Opportunity" for the new Millenium Hill, Franklin; Cohen, Sarah www.Schoolfacilities.com 2005
- Feng Shui for the Classroom: 101 easy to Use Ideas Heiss, Renee Zephyr Press, Chicago, 2004
- Volume, Scale and Shape Lang, Dale Christopher, University of Washington, 2003
- The Importance of Interior Design Elements as they Relate to Student Outcomes, Tanner. Kenneth; Langford, Ann, 2003 http://www.eric.ed.gov/ERICWebPortal/custom/portlets/recordDetails/detailmini.jsp?_nfpb=true&_&ERICExtSearch_SearchValue_0=ED478177&ERICExtSearch_SearchType_0=no&accno=ED478177
- Classrooms of the Future: Thinking Out of the Box Lackney, Jeffery A Sept '04 http://schoolstudio.engr.wisc.edu/futureclassrooms.html
- Multipurpose Spaces http://www.edfacilities.org/pubs/
- Electronic Classrooms and Buildings of the Future http://www.educause.edu/ir/library/pdf/EDU0074.pdf
- Designing for All Children Stoecklin, Vicki 1999 http://www.whitehutchinson.com/children/articles/designforall.shtml
- Learning Environments and Classroom Design Sturt Gary http://www.edfacilities.org/rl/classroom_design.cfm
- Shared Visions? Architects and Teachers Perceptions on the Design of Classroom Environments Horne, Sandra Loughborough University, UK http://www.lboro.ac.uk/departments/cd/docs_dandt/idater/downloads98/horne98.pdf
- Leading the Transition from Classrooms to Learning Spaces Oblinger, Diana Educause;v28 n1; Oct 2005 http://educause.edu/apps/eq/eqm05/eqm0512.asp?bhcp=1
- Classrooms and their Impact on Learning Gardner, Dwayne School Planning and Management; v44 n2,p44,42; Feb 2005
- Let the Walls Teach Chan, Tak Cheung; Arasi, Anthony School Business Affairs; v71 n1,p35,36; Jan 2005
- The L-Shape Classroom: A Pattern for Promoting Learning Lippman, Peter C. DesignShare; p9; Oct 2004 http://www.designshare.com/index.php/articles/the-l-shaped-classroom/
- Creating Blueprints for Literacy: Simple Ideas for designing a Literacy-Friendly Head Start Classroom Denham, Marty Children and families; v8 n1, 28-30; Winter 1999
- Parents Speak Out: What Should Schools and Classrooms Look Like? Foster-Harrison, Elizabeth S; Peel, Henry A Schools I the Middle; v7 n1, p42-47; Sept-Oct 1997
- Classroom Design and How it Influences Behaviour Colbert, Judith Early Childhood News; v9 n3, p22-29;May-Jun 1997
- Psychological Aspects of Classroom Planning White, Ernest K CEFP Journal; v28 n5; Sep-Oct 1990
- Designs for Living and Learning: Transforming Early Childhood Environments, Deb Curtis and Margie Carter

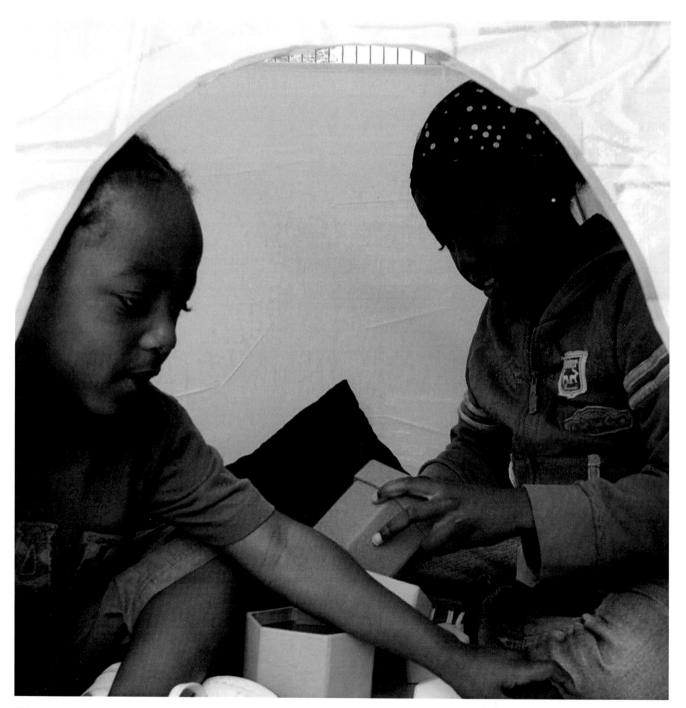